Climbing the Church Wall

Rob Portlock

Author of
Off the Church Wall and *Way Off the Church Wall*

INTERVARSITY PRESS
DOWNERS GROVE, ILLINOIS 60515

© 1991 by Rob Portlock

All rights reserved. No part of this book may be reproduced in any form without written permission from InterVarsity Press, P.O. Box 1400, Downers Grove, Illinois 60515.

InterVarsity Press is the book-publishing division of InterVarsity Christian Fellowship, a student movement active on campus at hundreds of universities, colleges and schools of nursing in the United States of America, and a member movement of the International Fellowship of Evangelical Students. For information about local and regional activities, write Public Relations Dept., InterVarsity Christian Fellowship, 6400 Schroeder Rd., P.O. Box 7895, Madison, WI 53707-7895.

Cover illustration: Rob Portlock

ISBN 0-8308-1830-8

Printed in the United States of America ∞

Library of Congress Cataloging-in-Publication Data

Portlock, Rob.
    Climbing the church walls/Rob Portlock.
      p.   cm.
    ISBN 0-8308-1830-8
    1. Christian life—Caricatures and cartoons.   2. American wit and
humor, Pictorial. I. Title.
NC1429.P65A4 1991
741.5'973—dc20   *91-17872*
                                  CIP

15	14	13	12	11	10	9	8	7	6	5	4	3	2	1
03	02	01	00	99	98	97	96	95	94	93	92	91		

Introduction

Close to where we live there's a store that has nothing but music boxes. Dozens and dozens of music boxes. As you wander through the store and open each small lid, a song comes from within. Each song stirs some emotion or memory. I hope the cartoons in this book stir some funny emotion or memory for you.

Rob Portlock

"Of course, on the other hand, . . ."

"Now, while Brother Watson is finishing his prayer, let's turn to hymn number . . ."

Calvary Church finally came up with a solution for the sleeping-leg syndrome.

"I still think he could do more for the church."

PORTLOCK

"My agent and I have decided that if I don't get my own dressing room, you'll have to find yourself a new Mary."

"I'm glad to present our new choir. They're a little shy."

Sunday, Sept. 20. I'm worried. Third Sunday with no "Amens" during my sermon.

"Well, Dad, you said to pray for anything I wanted!"

"We need fifteen thousand big ones. No questions asked."

"You're going to have to cut down on salt, fatty foods, and fire and brimstone sermons."

"Now, Mr. Perkins, if you would, step up to the mike and do your best rendition of 'Louie, Louie.'"

"My sermon today is from First Peter, chapter three: 'Wives, be subject to your husbands.'"

"Could you renew Dexter for me?"

The day Pastor Bob and the board decided to give a rapture exhibition.

"They have a way of singling out non-tithers!"

"Once a year he likes to play shepherd and sheep."

"Have I ever told you the parable of the man who left his keys at home?"

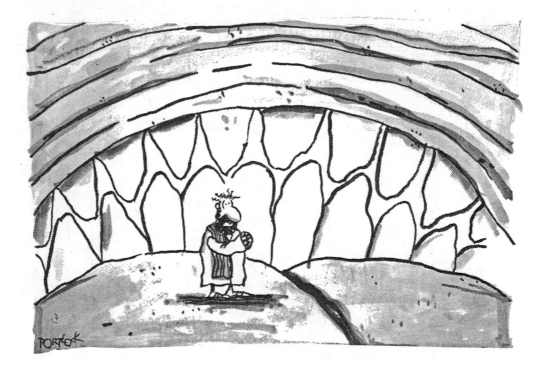

Jonah. The first "save the whales" advocate.

"We don't know what you're doing in here, but we've been waiting five minutes to talk to you about the broken hand dryer in the ladies' room."

"I'd like to thank the board for the lovely plant after our disagreement this week."

"Who'd ever have thought you'd need 3-D glasses to see here?"

"If I'm not mistaken, we hired our beloved pastor in 1989."

"I think he's taken this 'humbler than thou' thing to its limit."

Usher Ed "Ten-Dollar Minimum Tithe" Smith

"Noah, the elephants are acting up again!"

"Our speaker tonight is Bob Wilson, a missionary to the city of Memphis."

...SMITHS up 3% ... JONES down 9% ... HAWKINS down 5% ... HERNANDEZ up 7% ...

PASTOR

PORTLOK

TITHING TICKER

"I think it's time we had a talk with the pastor about his priorities."

"I don't know about you, but I don't care for the new usher uniforms."

"See, Fred, I told you it was Pre-Trib."

Choir at restaurant after church service.

"Yes, I was a Christian bookstore owner. Why do you ask?"

"See, I told you the offering would be bigger if we played 'I'm Busted' during the collection."

"Your assistant pastor is going to overthrow you."

"Excuse me. I'm allergic to clouds."

"Hi, I'm the new youth pastor. We always have room for a big, bad wolf in our youth group."

"This suit has just enough of the humble servant, smart theologian, dynamic minister look—
and not an ounce of televangelist."

PORTLOK

"And then, when I was two years old . . ."

"I still say Counselor Smith is on a 'power trip.'"

"Pssst, gold closed at $496.20 so I had to use my sister's necklace."

"That's what the youth group came up with for a witnessing tool."

"No! No! No! For the thousandth time, Elvis is *not* still alive on earth!"

"Now, make like Paul."

"Have you noticed anything different about Wilbur lately?"

"This copyrighted broadcast is brought to you solely for the noncommercial use of our audience. Any rebroadcast, reproduction, or use of any of the descriptions and accounts of this service, without the express written consent of the Reverend will result in an ugly scandalous national lawsuit."

"Pastor, just thought we'd let you see the carpet we picked for the youth hall!"

Usher Claude decides to find out for himself if any of the nontithing parishioners
have anything to give.

"Pastor Harry thinks sinners and hamburgers have the same fate. Fire and Brimstone."

"Before we start this counseling session, I'd like to introduce my lawyers, Wallace, Van Patten, Jones & Beck, Inc."

"My sermon today is 'Why you shouldn't read the Dow Jones Average.'"

"So how was the board meeting, honey?"

PORTLOCK

"I wish I'd never bought him that book on shepherding!"

"Ouch!"

"Get me the contractor on the phone!"

"I'm sorry, Paul. You've just jumped around too much."

The church of the 90s should be interesting.

PORLOCK

"Today my sermon is on joy."

"Of course we'll accept your check, but we'll need a driver's license, major credit card, your mother's maiden name, a thumb print and blood sample, and you'll have to leave your firstborn until the check clears."

"Don't you get it, Baxter? You don't have to do that here."

"That solves our usher problem."

"Mom and Dad, they chose me to be the star of the Christmas play!"

"I think he's becoming too preoccupied with the Second Coming."

"I think we ordered the wrong cupola!"

"They like to make a quick exit here."

"My text for today is the first three words in the Bible . . . 'genuine Moroccan leather.' "

"You don't understand. I'm Harrison R. Bentley II, and I *can* take it with me."

"We thought we'd find you here. The potluck committee wanted to get your permission to change from a floral-pattern napkin to a generic brand."

"After studying our financial records for the past year, we suspect one of you ushers is skimming some of the offerings."

"I had a vision that this church isn't supposed to watch any of the top ten TV programs."

"No, Pastor Smith, it's 'Spring forward, fall back!' "

"I can support a church softball and volleyball team, but I cannot support a church wrestling team."